© Editorial Playor

Adapted and published in the
United States in 1985 by
Silver Burdett Company,
Morristown, New Jersey

1985 Printing

ISBN 0-382-09094-2   (Lib. Bdg)
ISBN 0-382-09100-0

Library of Congress
Catalog Card Number 85-40431

Silver Burdett Company

# CLASSICS FOR KIDS

# THE BALLAD OF EL CID

*Adapted for young readers by Vincent Buranelli*

*illustrated by Hieronimus Fromm*

Rodrigo Diaz de Vivar was called "El Cid." This means "The Hero" in Spanish. He was a knight from Castile, in Spain, and a skillful and brave warrior. He served his lord, King Alfonso, with great respect and loyalty.

But El Cid's enemies succeeded in turning the king against him. The king ordered El Cid to leave his kingdom. The good Cid, followed by his knights, was forced to leave his castle and ride into exile.

When El Cid and his knights were passing through the city of Burgos, they saw that the people of the town were standing at their windows to see them pass.

The people were sad, and many wept to see El Cid leave. But they could do nothing for him, for the king had forbidden anyone to give him shelter or sell him food.

El Cid felt unhappy as he left Burgos. He would like to have stayed there, but he knew that if he did, the king would punish the people. So, El Cid rode through Burgos without stopping.

Later, when El Cid camped outside the city, a man by the name of Martin Antolinez approached him and his knights and offered them food.

Antolinez was not disobeying the king, for he did not sell the food, but chose to give it to them. Antolinez did this because he admired El Cid.

El Cid needed money to continue on his way, and feed his men. Antolinez had a plan. He filled two glittering and costly chests with sand, and took them to some merchants in Burgos.

He told them that they were filled with all of El Cid's money and valuables, and that El Cid was not allowed to leave the king's lands with them. He offered to allow them to keep the chests in exchange for 600 gold and silver coins, provided they did not open the chests for a year.

The merchants accepted, thinking they had made an excellent deal. They were greedy, and they were tricked because of their greed.

El Cid and his knights continued on their way. Finally, they reached a monastery where El Cid's wife, Donna Jimena, and his daughters, Sol and Elvira, were staying.

Before leaving the kingdom, El Cid wanted to say good-bye to his family. They were all sad because he had to go. He could not stay with them because the monastery was within the kingdom.

After leaving his family, El Cid and his knights continued on their journey. Many men joined him. They all wanted to ride with the brave knight, El Cid.

He led his followers to the end of the kingdom, where the land of the Moors began. The Moors had invaded Spain from North Africa. The Spaniards were trying to drive them out.

El Cid and his knights fought the Moors, to reconquer the land that the Moors had occupied. The battles were long and hard, for the Moors were also valiant warriors.

For more than three years, El Cid and his knights continued fighting battles and defeating the Moors. They took more and more Spanish lands back from the invaders.

El Cid led his men all the way to the shores of the Mediterranean. There stood the great city of Valencia. El Cid knew he must capture Valencia if Spain was to throw off Moorish rule. There were many battles between Spaniards and Moors on the ramparts of Valencia.

El Cid and his knights were able to take Valencia after a long struggle. Along with the victory, his men reaped many riches. But El Cid remembered with sadness that the king, whom he still wanted to serve, was angry with him. The king still considered El Cid an enemy.

To show his loyalty, El Cid took one hundred beautiful horses his army had seized in Valencia and sent them to King Alfonso. The messenger who brought the horses to the king told him of the many brave deeds of El Cid.

King Alfonso now agreed that El Cid was his faithful servant. The king asked him to return, and ordered that his lands be given back to him.

There were two Princes of Carrion—Fernando and Diego Gonzalez—who were very ambitious. They pleaded with the king to persuade El Cid to allow them to marry his daughters.

The princes wanted to increase their power and wealth by being related to Spain's greatest knight. El Cid agreed to the marriage of his daughters.

The wedding ceremony was celebrated with a great banquet. The followers of the king and the knights of El Cid feasted together. The daughters of El Cid, Elvira and Sol, sat beside their new husbands, Fernando and Diego Gonzalez.

But these two Princes of Carrion were not to be trusted. They were liars, and cowards as well. They just pretended to be truthful and brave.

One afternoon, while El Cid slept, a lion escaped from his cage. The Princes of Carrion, who were cowards, ran away, leaving their wives unprotected.

At that moment, El Cid woke up and faced the lion, forcing it back into its cage. Everyone made fun of the princes for their cowardice. They became angry, and fled. Then they abandoned their wives, who were El Cid's daughters.

El Cid asked the king for justice. The king decided that the Princes of Carrion should fight against two soldiers from El Cid's army. The soldiers easily defeated the cowardly princes. El Cid was then fortunate, for two other young princes who were very brave came and asked to marry his daughters.

They were wed, and from then on, El Cid, and his wife Donna Jimena lived happily as lord and lady of Valencia. They enjoyed the respect and trust of their king.

1 2 3 4 5 6 7 8 9 10—JDL—90 89 88 87 86 85